DISCARD

D1377352

Teens and Phobias

Other titles in the *Teen Mental Health* series include:

Teens and ADHD
Teens and Eating Disorders
Teens and Gender Dysphoria
Teens and OCD
Teens and PTSD
Teens and Suicide

Teens and Phobias

Bitsy Kemper

ReferencePoint
Press®

San Diego, CA

© 2017 ReferencePoint Press, Inc.
Printed in the United States

For more information, contact:
ReferencePoint Press, Inc.
PO Box 27779
San Diego, CA 92198
www.ReferencePointPress.com

LIBRARY OF CONGRESS CATALOGING-IN-PUBLICATION DATA

Name: Kemper, Bitsy, author.
Title: Teens and phobias / by Bitsy Kemper.
Description: San Diego, CA : ReferencePoint Press, Inc., 2017. | Series: Teen mental health series | Includes bibliographical references and index.
Identifiers: LCCN 2016035298 (print) | LCCN 2016035774 (ebook) | ISBN 9781682821282 (hardback) | ISBN 9781682821299 (eBook)
Subjects: LCSH: Phobias in children--Juvenile literature.
Classification: LCC RJ506.P38 K46 2017 (print) | LCC RJ506.P38 (ebook) | DDC 618.92/85225--dc23
LC record available at https://lccn.loc.gov/2016035298

CONTENTS

Real Fear, Real Problem

H arry Potter, afraid of clowns?

Daniel Radcliffe, the actor famous for playing Harry Potter in the Harry Potter movie series, is a coulrophobe. That means he is afraid of clowns. He is not the only one. There is no official data about how many teens suffer from coulrophobia, but an estimated 12 percent of adults in the United States suffer from it. Radcliffe is one of the most famous coulrophobes. Actor Johnny Depp suffers from coulrophobia too. It has also been reported that megafamous rapper and music producer Sean "P. Diddy" Combs was so scared of clowns that he had a strict no-clown clause in his performance agreements.

It might seem surprising that anyone—famous or otherwise—could be so concerned about some silly person in makeup who is supposed to be making kids laugh. But it is no laughing matter to those who suffer from this phobia. It can cause a state of panic, difficulty in breathing, irregular heartbeat, sweating, nausea, feelings of fear, and maybe even screaming and crying. The fear of clowns can be downright debilitating. It might prevent someone from ever eating inside a McDonald's. They will never shop in a party goods store. Not knowing when a clown or a clown image may crop up on billboards, television, or around town can keep a person anxious and uncomfortable at all times. As trivial as it may seem, a clown phobia should not be treated lightly. No phobia should.

A Disconnect in the Brain

"Phobia," according to the Mayo Clinic, "is an overwhelming and unreasonable fear of an object or situation that poses little real danger but provokes anxiety and avoidance."[1] Phobias are not just fleeting fears; they are long-lasting, and they cause intense—and often disruptive—physical and psychological reactions. There are many types of phobias—and they are not uncommon. The American Psychiatric Association reports that about 5 percent of children and 16 percent of adolescents will develop a phobia. Studies find that more kids have phobias than adults, and girls are more than twice as likely as boys to experience a phobia. According to the National Institute of Mental Health, over six hundred thousand teenagers in the United States suffer from anxiety disorders such as phobias. Many of them suffer in silence, too embarrassed to tell anyone.

In a sense, phobias are an outgrowth of normal brain behavior. When one senses danger, the brain reacts instantly, sending signals that activate the nervous system. This happens in any brain, phobic or not. It causes physical responses, such as a faster heartbeat, rapid breathing, and an increase in blood pressure. Blood pumps to muscle groups to prepare the body for physical action, such as running or fighting. As psychologist Andrea Umbach puts it, "Fear is an emotion that gets the body moving in order to avoid danger."[2] The entire body is placed on high alert. Skin starts to form beads of sweat to keep the body cool. Sensations like tingling and shaking are sent to the stomach, head, chest, legs, or hands. These physical sensations of fear can be mild or strong. For the most part, the brain is able to assess the level of danger and match the symptoms to it. The brain and body are engineered to keep one safe.

> "Fear is an emotion that gets the body moving in order to avoid danger."[2]
>
> —Psychologist Andrea Umbach

But for the phobic brain, there is a disconnect. The "on" switch stays on too long, and is clicked too often, in situations where there is no real danger. People with phobias finds themselves too often stuck in survival mode. And once fear is engaged, the body's reaction can be very hard to shut down.

In the case of coulrophobia, it turns out that the person is probably really afraid of not knowing who the person is behind the makeup. Depp admits that it is "something about the painted face,

Fear of clowns is just one of many phobias that afflict young people. Experts estimate that 5 percent of children and 16 percent of adolescents will develop some type of phobia.

the fake smile. There always seemed to be a darkness lurking just under the surface, a potential for real evil."[3] That is why it is common for coulrophobes to also fear people dressed up with fake beards and mustaches, such as Santa Claus. Maybe they associate clowns with unpleasant circus mischief. The fear could have been triggered by a traumatic childhood event. But why they are afraid does not matter at all. Phobias, in general, are not rational. The fears—and all the related symptoms that arise from them— are real, even if the character behind the makeup is not.

Many Teens Suffer in Silence

People with phobias have several battles to fight when face-to-face with what they fear most. They have the physical struggles of anxiety and fear, such as shortness of breath, butterflies in their stomach, and weak knees. They also have the internal struggles of anxiety and fear, such as "I am so scared!" or "I should run!" At the same time, they may be thinking, "This is stupid. I know I shouldn't be afraid!" or "I am so afraid right now that I want to run away, but my knees are shaking and I'm so scared that I can't move!"

Emotionally, phobias take another toll. Many phobic teens often suffer in silence. They are too afraid to admit their fear. They do not want to be laughed at. They do not want to be teased. They do not want to be bullied. Mostly, they are too embarrassed to admit their fear. Their flushed cheeks and sweat might be obvious, but internal shakes and wild thoughts might not be. Symptoms may only be observed by the sufferer. External symptoms might be purposely masked by someone who is not willing to admit his or her fear. A passerby may not notice at all.

Many teens would rather suffer the consequences of the phobia than suffer the consequences of someone finding out about it. With a less common phobia like the fear of clowns, teens know their friends are sure to laugh it off and not take it seriously. Admitting a phobia of any kind puts a teen at risk for being made fun of or for feeling vulnerable. Teens are therefore less likely to admit their fears to anyone. By hiding their fear, no one knows they are suffering or in pain. But by denying their phobia, they are unable to get the help they need to overcome their fear. And that is unfortunate. Most phobias will not go away on their own. Intervention of some sort, whether through counseling or medication, is almost always required. "Phobics are easily embarrassed, but recovery *requires* that others find out about their phobias," says Dr. Fredric Neuman. As director of the Anxiety and Phobia Treatment Center, he has seen the positive effects of therapy. The anxiety and phobia expert stresses the need for professional help because phobias do not go away overnight, even with assistance. "Practicing to overcome

"Something about the painted face, the fake smile. There always seemed to be a darkness lurking just under the surface, a potential for real evil."[3]

—Johnny Depp, actor and coulrophobe

a phobia takes time, sometimes a lot of time. And repetition,"[4] Neuman adds.

Another reason why keeping the secret is detrimental is that it keeps the person farther and farther away from healing. People who fear clowns, for example, want to avoid clowns at all costs. They understandably will not go anywhere near one. It is the same for any sort of phobia, whether it is a fear of needles or heights or public speaking. Individuals who are afraid want to avoid what they fear. It seems logical. What they do not understand, because they have not gotten any professional help, is that avoidance is exactly the wrong thing to do. A better approach is to face the fear, little by little, to overcome it one step at a time. Only with the guided help of a professional, and maybe medication, are they able to be cured of the fear. Unfortunately, they will not know that until they schedule their first meeting with a health professional. And they will not do that until they admit they have a problem. Luckily, there is virtually no phobia that cannot be controlled or cured. All it takes is someone willing to face the fear and work on making the phobia go away.

> "Phobics are easily embarrassed, but recovery *requires* that others find out about their phobias."[4]
>
> —Dr. Fredric Neuman, director of the Anxiety and Phobia Treatment Center

CHAPTER ONE

What Are Phobias?

Fear is normal and necessary. Human survival is based on it. When sensing danger, the brain reacts instantly, kicking the nervous system into high alert. This causes physical responses, like a faster heartbeat and shorter, more rapid breathing. Blood quickly pumps to muscles to prepare the body to either fight or run. Beads of sweat form on the skin to keep the body cool. The stomach flips, feet and arms tingle, and the head gets light. The mind creates physical reactions in the body within milliseconds.

This is known as a fight-or-flight response because the body is preparing to do exactly that: either get ready to stay put and fight off the danger (fight) or run like mad to get away (flight). The body stays in this fight-or-flight state until the brain gets an all-clear safety message that the danger is gone. Only then does it turn off the fear reaction. The fight-or-flight response is instinctual, meaning it happens without the person in danger even knowing it.

Fear's emotional response to the dangerous situation has physical effects. It is designed to keep creatures of all kinds safe. And it has served humankind well. Someone who is afraid of getting sick, for example, probably will not hug or shake hands with someone who has the flu. That fear keeps the person away from known germ-ridden situations and helps him or her stay healthy—and alive.

A little kid might fear strangers or the dark. Older kids might fear thunder or their first day of school. The fear might be hidden, or it might be obvious. According to the Child Anxiety Network, an online health resource for child anxiety, the most common fears of kids ages seven to sixteen include injury, illness, school performance, death, and natural disasters. Through learning and experience, and with help from adults, most teens are able to outgrow and conquer these fears.

But what if the fear does not go away? What if a young person becomes *more* afraid? When a fear becomes extreme and unmanageable, it is considered a phobia. A phobia is fear on a whole different level. In an article titled "Childhood Fears and Anxieties," the respected newsletter *Harvard Medical School Mental Health Letter* explains it this way:

> Any of the common childhood fears, and many others, can become clinically significant phobias if they are severe enough, persist long enough, or occur at an inappropriate age. Phobias in children come and go rapidly up to the age of 10, and they do not usually require treatment unless there are other symptoms, such as excessive general anxiety or refusal to go to school.[5]

Adult support and help is needed in order to get over phobias; they rarely go away on their own.

Fear Versus Phobia

When a fear grows to the point that it is out of proportion with the possible danger, becomes excessive or unrealistic, and interferes with daily life, it is considered a phobia. A phobia is an intense fear reaction to a particular thing or situation that poses little or no real danger. A person with a phobia may even realize that his or her fear is unreasonable yet still cannot control it.

A phobia will not go away by trying to calm the person down or by saying, "It's okay, there's nothing to be afraid of." A kid with a fear of heights is not going to stop being afraid because a friend points out that he is only halfway up the ladder. Logic and a hug will not make that phobia go away on the spot.

"Any of the common childhood fears, and many others, can become clinically significant phobias if they are severe enough, persist long enough, or occur at an inappropriate age."[5]

—Harvard Medical School

It is not always easy to tell the difference between a fear and phobia. Many fears are normal. A person who cannot swim, for instance, might fear being in water. But when fear is ongoing and prevents one from going about daily life, it is considered a phobia. Using the same example, if the person who cannot swim refuses to attend a backyard barbecue in a home with a swimming pool out of fear of falling into the pool, that is a phobia.

Differences Between Fears and Phobias

Fears	Phobias
Feelings of angst while on a top floor of a tall building.	Turning down a job because it's in a skyscraper.
Tension when a larger dog approaches you on a walk.	Avoiding the park because you might see a dog.
Nervousness during takeoff on an airplane.	Not going on a family vacation because you'd have to fly to the destination.

Source: Gabe Duverge, "Persistent Fears: Exploring the Science Behind Phobias," Notre Dame College Online, April 30, 2015. http://online.notredamecollege.edu.

The emotional and physical reactions that fear creates, like racing thoughts and sweat, might be just the beginning for phobia sufferers. For them, fear responses are activated too frequently, too strongly, and in situations where such responses are out of place. Because the physical sensations that go with the response are real, the danger feels very real too. The person might react by freezing up or running away.

Anxiety Disorders

Phobias are a type of anxiety disorder. People with anxiety disorders experience fear and powerlessness and, often, a sense of doom or impending danger. The National Institute of Mental Health reports that phobias affect almost 10 percent of adults.

The Fear of Using Public Toilets

The American Urological Association estimates that one in four Americans suffers from so-called shy bladder, or paruresis, which is the difficulty to urinate in the presence of others. Teens with this fear have to use a private restroom, not just a private stall, to go the bathroom. Others have to wait until they get home. This phobia, which usually starts in the teenage years, may lead to kids cutting back on their social life so they do not have to use bathrooms away from home.

In 2015 a sixteen-year-old girl in England died from complications directly traced back to her refusal to use public toilets for two months. Her bowels became obstructed, which led to a heart attack. Since this topic is rarely talked about openly, teens who have this phobia often believe they are the only ones suffering from it. They feel ashamed and become expert at hiding it from their friends, parents, and doctors. The sense of shame and depression can be a lot to handle. And it prevents teens from getting help.

Clinical psychologist Edmund J. Bourne, an expert in anxiety and phobias, estimates that anxiety disorders have now risen to affect about 40 million people between the ages of eighteen and sixty-five. The US Department of Health and Human Services indicates that as many as thirteen in every one hundred children have an anxiety disorder. Stats on teen phobias are harder to pin down, with many doctors pointing to the difficulty teens have admitting—and therefore reporting—their fears. Many teens are simply too embarrassed to tell anyone they are afraid.

Dr. E. Jane Costello of Duke University's Center for Child and Family Policy thinks the difficulty in finding stats on teens could also be because teen emotional conditions are not taken as seriously as they should be and are undertreated. By denying or not reporting their phobia, teens are not able to get the help they need to get over their fear. In one study, Costello found only one in five children with a serious mental health disorder received services. "We need to train more child psychiatrists in this country," Costello said. "And those individuals need to be used strategically, as consultants to the school counselors."[6]

It might take years for someone suffering from a phobia to admit to the problem, longer still before admitting to anyone else that he or she needs help, and even longer before seeking professional assistance. The American Academy of Child & Adolescent Psychiatry reports that about 40 percent of social phobia sufferers have symptoms for over ten years before seeking help. Since many phobias can start during childhood and the teen years, it is important to address them early on. But how does one know if expert help is needed?

It is considered normal to have anxiety before a big test, to be nervous when asking a friend out to dinner, to fear skydiving, and to feel uncomfortable at a party where everyone is a stranger. When anxiety and fear become extreme and detrimental, such as not being able to eat or sleep for two nights before taking *any* test, it is considered abnormal. Any time a phobia gets in the way of everyday life, it is time for intervention.

Social Phobia

The most common teen phobia, according to the Mayo Clinic, is social phobia. It typically starts in early tween or teen years, a time when feeling accepted by peers is very important. Social phobia typically develops by age thirteen. The National Institute of Mental Health found that 1 in 8 teenagers suffers from this form of severe shyness. It is one of the most common anxiety disorders in adults, and the experts at Massachusetts General Hospital say it affects at least 1 percent of children. They note that the number may be higher because children's symptoms may incorrectly be attributed to a shy personality.

The depth and impact of social phobia is often misunderstood. Some think it is a simple preference to be alone. Filmmaker Woody Allen has joked, "I'm not anti-social, I'm just not social."[7] But being antisocial is different than being afraid of social situations. Social phobia, also called social anxiety, is more than just being too shy to speak up in a group. It is more than being uncomfortable meeting new people or not knowing how to engage in small talk. Social phobia is a type of anxiety problem.

Extreme feelings of shyness and self-consciousness build up into a powerful fear that makes a teen feel uncomfortable in everyday social situations. General characteristics of social phobias include blushing, sweating, trembling or shaking, nausea or upset stomach, shaky voice and difficulty talking, increased heartbeat, and difficulty making or keeping eye contact.

"Social phobias involve a combination of excessive self-consciousness and a fear of public scrutiny or humiliation in common social situations. The teen fears being rejected. They fear being viewed or judged negatively, and they fear offending others,"[8] says California-based licensed marriage and family therapist Nancy Milla. Someone with social phobia will let that fear rule their calendar. Instead of enjoying sports or parties or meeting friends at the mall, a teen with social phobia might dread them—and avoid them altogether. This can be dangerous as well as isolating. Anne Marie Albano, director of the Columbia University Clinic for Anxiety and Related Disorders at the Columbia University Medical Center, notes that kids with social anxiety disorders are more likely to develop depression by age fifteen and substance abuse issues by age sixteen or seventeen, compared to teens without the disorder.

The Fear of Public Speaking

One type of social phobia is the fear of public speaking. Speaking or presenting in front of an audience is probably the greatest and most common social phobia in teenagers. Study after study shows that many people fear public speaking even more than they fear death.

With teens, any situation involving speaking or performing in front of or with a group—especially if it involves being the center of attention—can cause this fear. Some teens might not be able to concentrate in class because they are afraid the teacher might call on them. This phobia can even affect student athletes, artists, and performers—some of whom develop such extreme performance anxiety that they lose sleep, get sick before starting their performance, perform poorly, or refuse to perform altogether.

Anxiety disorders are the most common mental illnesses in the United States and specific phobias—that is, phobias involving particular objects, animals, or even bodily functions—are the most common anxiety disorder, according to the Anxiety and Depression Association of America. People with specific phobias exhibit fear of a particular object or situation that is out of proportion to the actual risk. This type of phobia often begins in childhood, between the ages of seven and eleven, and continues into the teenage years and sometimes into adulthood.

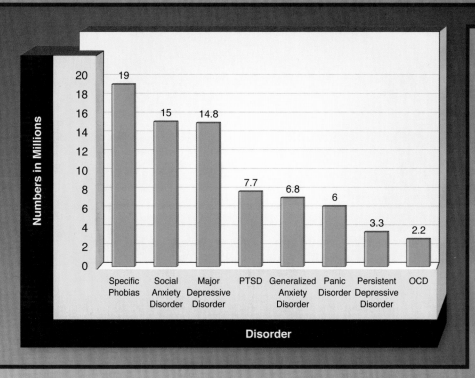

Number of Americans Suffering From:

Source: Anxiety and Depression Association of America, "Facts and Statistics," September 2014. www.adaa.org.

Singer Adele admits to getting so nervous before concerts that she has had anxiety attacks and has thrown up beforehand. One of the top-selling recording artists of all time, Adele reportedly does not like live venues but has learned to manage her

Grammy award-winning singer Adele says she feels so nervous before a live performance that she sometimes has anxiety attacks and throws up. She has learned to manage her phobia so that she can perform on stage.

phobia enough to enable her to perform on stage. Even Mahatma Gandhi, considered one of India's greatest political leaders, was said to have run from a room out of embarrassment while trying his first case as a lawyer in front of a judge. On one occasion he completely froze up while talking to a small group. And yet, he too, was able to curb his phobia.

In their cases, and in almost all social phobia cases, the significance of the performance is irrelevant. The size of the crowd does not matter. It can be filled with strangers or friends. The fear lies in being the center of attention within a group of people, even if the group is a fan base. Adele's and Gandhi's anxieties were classified as social phobias, instead of fears, because they were excessive. Both icons needed help to overcome performance anxiety in order for them to continue on to success.

Being in front of a group may cause many underlying fears to surface. There could be a fear that the anxiety is noticeable by others. The fear that someone will notice a red face or sweat might make the face redden even more or make the sweat worsen. But more than that is the fear of making a mistake and then being judged or found inadequate. In a nutshell, it is the fear of being a failure in front of the group.

> "I want to have a relationship. I want to kiss and get my heart broken and call someone baby. But I just can't. I'm afraid. I panic sometimes. My fears are ruining my life."[9]
>
> —A teen girl suffering from social phobia

The Fear of Dating

Another type of social phobia that is common among teens is the fear of dating. This is the fear of asking for a date and being asked on a date, but it also includes the fear of meeting people of the opposite sex. It can also include the fear of sharing personal information, which can affect the development of a relationship. A sixteen-year-old girl describes her fear of dating this way:

> Guys try to talk to me on the street and I ignore them, even if I think they are cute. If guys try to make eye contact, I look the other way. My friend wanted to hang out but I've only hung out with her in group settings so I lied and told her I was busy. I mean what if we hung out and guys approached us, and I couldn't handle the situation. I want to have a relationship. I want to kiss and get my heart broken and call someone baby. But I just can't. I'm afraid. I panic sometimes. My fears are ruining my life.[9]

Specific Phobias

Teens can also experience phobias that involve particular objects or animals or even specific bodily functions. These are known as specific phobias. Specific phobias involve an unreasonable fear of a specific object or situation that is out of proportion to the actual risk. People with the specific phobia known as arachnophobia—the fear of spiders—might not just fear a tiny spider climbing up a water spout. Simply seeing a photo of a spider might be enough to make them scream. They understand that the spider on the page is an image, not real. Yet the sufferer might feel the same emotional and physical fear as if the spider were alive and crawling.

The Anxiety Disorders Association of British Columbia has found that specific phobias begin in childhood, between the ages of seven to eleven, with most cases starting before age ten. The disorder might be the direct result of a specific or perceived traumatic occurrence. For example, teen Brianna Morley was working at a zoo camp when a young camper vomited. All she could do was wonder if it would happen again, to the point that it got in the way of her work. "My goal was always to work with the kids, but now I just feel so anxious and jumpy I'm not sure if I could do it. It makes me really want to get over this phobia,"[10] she says. Brianna created a blog about emetophobia, which is the fear of vomiting. She reached out to other teens to see if anyone else felt the same way. She made YouTube videos about it, and her blog encourages other teens to seek help as she has.

There are many other specific phobias covering a range of fears. They include the fear of lightning; the fear of blood, injection, or medical procedures like dental work; and the fear of colors. Specific phobias that are common among teenagers include the fear of taking tests and the fear of being without one's phone.

The Fear of Taking Tests

Test anxiety is not just getting nervous before a big test. Testophobia, as it is known, causes people to fear that no matter how well they have studied and know the test material, they simply will not be able to remember it for an exam. Kids with test anxiety can suffer from both physical and mental pains. The brain latches

Rare Phobias

Health experts have identified hundreds of phobias. Although some are fairly common, many are so rare that they affect 0.000000001 percent or less of the population. Below is a list of phobias that, although rare, have nevertheless been documented in medical literature.

arachibutyrophobia: The fear of peanut butter sticking to the roof of one's mouth.

asymmetriphobia: The fear of mismatched socks or asymmetrical objects.

aulophobia: The fear of flutes.

cathisophobia: The fear of sitting down.

chorophobia: The fear of dancing.

chromophobia: The fear of colors. Many colors have their own phobia name, such as rhodophobia, which is the fear of the color pink.

deipnophobia: The fear of dinner parties, dining, and dinner conversation.

dextrophobia: The fear of objects situated to the person's right.

didaskaleinophobia: The fear of going to school.

eisoptrophobia: The fear of one's own reflection.

ephebiphobia: The fear of teenagers.

lutraphobia: The fear of otters.

papyrophobia: The fear of paper.

phobophobia: The fear of having a phobia and the internal anxiety sensations associated with them.

selenophobia: The fear of the moon.

venustraphobia: The fear of beautiful women; also known as caligynephobia.

onto thoughts—"This it too hard!" or "What if I can't remember anything?"—which makes it hard to study or sleep. The lack of concentration and lack of rest can lead to side effects like headaches or shaky hands, which makes it even harder for the brain to focus on facts and test questions. As a result, low test scores are almost guaranteed. The fear is therefore solidified in the brain as being legitimate, making it harder to overcome the next time a test comes up.

A student who suffers from this phobia will likely experience thoughts of panic and failure by the time the test begins. The train of thought is on a one-way track, directed at negativity, and anxiety worsens. Research such as that reported by the University of Maryland Medical Center and the Clinical Research Unit for Anxiety and Depression in Australia shows that perfectionists are more likely to suffer from a range of anxiety disorders. According to the KidsHealth website, young people who worry a lot or who are perfectionists are more likely to have trouble with test anxiety. When they are pushing for a perfect score, these traits make it hard to accept mistakes. It is the fear of a poor grade that creates the anxiety in the first place.

The Fear of Being Separated from One's Phone

Some phobias have been around for generations. One relatively new specific phobia is known as nomophobia, which is short for *no-more-phone phobia* or *no-mobile-phone phobia.* Nomophobia is the anxiety associated with being without one's cell phone. This phobia is especially common among young people. The symptoms can be severe, including nervousness and even feeling physically ill. The *Diagnostic and Statistical Manual of Mental Disorders,* a standard guidebook used by mental health professionals, does not recognize nomophobia as a legitimate phobia yet, but many professionals are taking notice.

Cell phones have become such a standard part of daily life that, according to *Time* magazine, the average person checks his or her phone 110 times a day. A nomophobe, on the other hand, is an addict; he or she might check 900 times a day. Caglar Yildirim, an Iowa State University student who has studied nomophobia, explains that "nomophobes feel extremely anxious when their phones go dead, because they tend to have a strong desire to be available, to stay connected, to have information at their fingertips."[11]

A high school science student from South Dakota conducted her own study. She found that without their phones, teens had higher blood pressure and heart rates. The teen scientist, Kashfia Nehrin Rahman, found that 92 percent of the teens surveyed keep their smartphones turned on 24/7, and 73 percent have anxiety when their battery dies. The teens who took part in the study checked their phones about once every twenty-three minutes, and 37 percent admitted to using their phones while driving. This dependency not only raises overall stress levels but also can be dangerous.

Nomophobes are overly absorbed with their smartphones. They continuously check their phones for messages in the middle of conversations and activities (even while taking a shower), and they often drop or leave a task in the middle to reply to a text or notification. They become irritable, restless, and short-tempered if they do not have their phones within reach. Nomophobes are often sleep deprived from staying up late or waking up many times in the middle of the night to check their phones for notifications or texts. It is not necessary to have all symptoms in order to have the phobia. Any strong symptom, or combination of symptoms, that prevents a teen from consistently carrying on or completing tasks or holding conversations or a job may signal that help is needed.

The Fear of Being Trapped

A third category of phobias can be described as the fear of being caught in situations where one might feel helpless, trapped, or embarrassed. Agoraphobia, as it is known, occurs most frequently in the late teens and early adulthood. The National Institute of Mental Health estimates about 40 percent of agoraphobia cases are considered severe.

Teens dealing with agoraphobia might not like being left alone in social situations or might fear places from which it would be hard to escape, such as in a car or elevator. They might home in on safety issues, wondering, "Where is the nearest exit? If there's an emergency, will I be close enough to run to safety?" When planning a night out, they might focus on health or social issues, thinking, "What if I'm sick and need to run to the rest room, won't that be embarrassing?" Instead of thinking about how much fun prom will be, they may worry about panic attacks and where they can go for shelter should one occur.

A teen with agoraphobia might be afraid to leave the house. "It happens every morning like clockwork. The twenty-minute drive [is] a buildup to the explosion. Heat flushes my cheeks, as my breath comes in desperate gasps. My stomach is in knots while shame festers in my chest. I can't go to school, I tell my mom. I feel sick. I'm going to be sick,"[12] says K.E. Nave about the daily struggle to leave the house. Agoraphobia almost caused Nave to fail eighth grade.

It might not be easy for agoraphobes to articulate their exact fear, making the fear harder to overcome. Nave tried to explain it further by saying, "I'm afraid of people caring. I'm afraid of people not caring. I'm afraid of what my fellow students will do to me, what they could do to me. I'm terrified of the anticipated and the unanticipated."[13] It is the fear of fear that keeps kids like Nave at home instead of out hanging with friends.

Interestingly, the fear of open spaces can also involve small spaces like elevators. It is not the same as claustrophobia—the fear of enclosed spaces—but it can have a similar effect in that the sufferer is overly concerned with not having an exit route. Agoraphobes are concerned they will have a panic attack in the small space and be unable to escape. For example, fifteen-year-old Ben had a panic attack in an elevator. Since then, he has worried about having additional panic attacks in elevators, and he refuses to ride in any elevator, anywhere. It is not that he is afraid the elevator will not work. Nor is he afraid of heights. His agoraphobia, in this case the fear of not being able to have an exit route when his panic attack hits, is what drives his inability to go about everyday life.

From group settings to spiders, the many forms of phobias are as diverse as the population. It might be surprising yet also encouraging for suffering teens to learn that phobias are quite common. And, most importantly, that they are treatable.

> "I'm afraid of people caring. I'm afraid of people not caring."[13]
>
> —K.E. Nave, an agoraphobic teen

CHAPTER TWO

What Causes Phobias?

Many of the phobias experienced by children and teens can be linked to the fact that young minds have a lesser ability to reason. A toddler might fear strangers because only familiar faces have been proven caregivers so far. Young ones may fear loud noises because they associate those noises with a disciplinary time-out. As the mind learns, simpler fears are figured out and outgrown. As a child ages, any fears that linger tend to become more complex. It is not known why some fears turn into phobias. Scientists believe phobias, like other anxiety-based problems, develop because of a combination of four factors: observing role models, trauma, life experiences, and genetics.

Role Models

Children learn from their parents, caregivers, and other types of role models, such as older brothers and sisters. They learn by observing what those role models do and by imitating how they act. To keep them safe, adults frequently warn children. A parent might caution, "Don't play near the street. There are cars and it can be dangerous," "Don't pet strange dogs. Ask the owner first if they bite," or simply "You have to be careful." Children therefore learn to steer clear of potentially dangerous situations. But broader wordings of warnings can cause different, more harmful associations in a child's mind. Children who hear "Don't play outside—it's dangerous," or "Don't pet dogs—they bite," can come to believe the world is a dangerous place. They might not be able to distinguish a safe part of the outdoors, such as a fenced-in backyard, from a dangerous parking lot. They might not be given the chance to learn the difference between a friendly dog and an aggressive one, which might lead them to conclude all dogs are dangerous. The perspective that the world is something to be feared, taught by a trusted role model, is hard to change.

A child with a naturally shy temperament is already suspicious of potential dangers. Role models unknowingly confirm those fears by constantly telling the child to be careful. It worsens the fears that might have already been brewing. A child can grow up fearful and mistrustful of the world, therefore making him or her much less likely to go out and explore. Fear can make the child more prone to worrying, overly concerned with safety, and more likely to suffer from a phobia. "If a child is prone to anxiety," says Dr. Jamie Howard of the Child Mind Institute, "it's helpful to know it sooner and to learn the strategies to manage sooner."[14] How a parent handles anxiety or shyness is how a child learns to handle anxiety or shyness. This can cause problems if the parent is also suffering from social anxiety. The child is not presented with the right tools to learn how to handle social situations properly.

In this case, for example, a socially phobic adult might be unwittingly teaching a child to be socially phobic too. Role models and parents who are extremely shy themselves might unintentionally set an example that shy behavior is the norm. A parent who experiences severe shyness is likely to avoid social interactions like dinner parties or receptions. By doing that, his or her children learn that socializing is uncomfortable, distressing, and something to avoid. Because those children are not presented with common social situations, they are not given opportunities to learn how to interact with others at common events like birthday parties. They are handed a double setback from their role models: they learn phobic behavior through observation and imitation, and they are not given the chance to explore social interaction in safe settings.

Overprotective and Overly Critical Parents

Phobias might start if caregivers overprotect a child, especially one who is already shy. An overprotected child does not have a chance to get used to new experiences, new situations, or

new people. If kept away from all potentially harmful conditions, children do not learn how to navigate dangers on their own and protect themselves. Children's fears can grow because the fear is reinforced when they think they are not capable of protecting themselves. Parental warnings can become reality. The child starts to avoid anything that might result in danger—even when the risk of danger is low. Avoiding danger, and staying out of harm's way, convinces them the avoidance was a good choice. The brain has been convinced that safety can be achieved only by avoidance. That leads to more avoidance. For example, if a child is afraid of the vacuum cleaner, an overprotective parent will never vacuum when the child is around. When that happens, the child never has the chance to see that the vacuum is harmless. He or she never has the chance to face and overcome the fear. Instead, the vacuum remains a mysterious, loud machine

Young people who experience harsh and constant criticism from a parent tend to focus more on their mistakes than their achievements. This can become a trigger for anxiety—and phobia.

that hides in the closet. The parent thinks he or she is helping the child, but this behavior is hurting the child in the long run.

Another way role models can affect potential teen phobia is if they are overly critical or set unrealistically high standards. Kids that are raised with critical parents are never truly sure of their own self-worth. Those children suffer from ongoing self-doubt because they never feel as if they are good enough. Children of a critical parent spend a lot of energy trying to please their parents and win their approval. It makes the children insecure. Insecure kids tend to worry more and be more fearful in general.

Clinical psychologist Greg Hajcak Proudfit found that when parenting focuses on perfection, it has a powerful and persistent effect because it trains a child's brain to overly emphasize mistakes. Children who are exposed to harsh criticism learn to internalize parental feedback. Any form of negativity becomes a trigger for anxiety. "Of course, everybody makes mistakes," Proudfit says. "But if you're punishing yourself more or responding to your mistakes more than the next kid, then that may be the trajectory of risk that leads you into an anxiety disorder."[15]

A study by the *Journal of the American Academy of Child & Adolescent Psychiatry* found that more than 22 percent of students who were both socially avoidant and fearful developed social phobia. That insecurity and general fear can easily spill over into friendships and all other social situations outside of the home. Children of overly critical parents do not want to be criticized at all, whether by themselves or by others. Not wanting to fail, especially in front of others, the self-critical person restricts social outings and interactions. They avoid making friends and going to events outside of school. They also internalize the desire to be perfect in order to measure up to their parent's expectation. A self-critical child is a prime candidate for social phobia, testophobia, and possibly other phobias.

Trauma

Some teens develop a phobia after being exposed to a traumatic or frightening event. A concern could begin as a rational, natural reaction to a frightening event. But if the teen agonizes over the event or lacks the emotional skills to cope with or understand what took place, the fear could become exaggerated to the point that the brain holds onto the memory of that event. Holding onto the memory of a dangerous or frightening event is, in a sense, a survival mechanism in the brain. By retaining that memory, the individual might be able to avoid a similar situation in the future.

The trauma might extend beyond what is actually feared into something loosely related to the feared item. Pediatric psychologist Lynne Kenney explains that a child might be bitten by a white dog and then fear mashed potatoes or vanilla ice cream. "This can be regarded as an error by the brain," Kenney clarifies. "The brain over-responds to a variety of stimuli that are similar to the original event. If a child is not helped to understand the fear and the meaning of the worry, he may feel powerless and thus may worry more."[16] The trauma of being bitten by a white dog creates a larger association of things to fear that are the same color as the dog, not just the dog itself.

Trauma might include a bad reaction to a bee sting that resulted in a long and painful visit to the emergency room and extended healing time, some sort of humiliation or embarrassment in front of other people, or an accident like falling off a ladder. Trauma might combine a few of those situations, such as being overly embarrassed by having to attend school with a swollen face that resulted from the bee sting.

Phobia resulting from trauma does not have to be based on personal experience. Learning about or witnessing someone else's traumatic event can also cause fear. If significant enough, the brain will save the memory of the fearful emotion for a long time. The effects will cause the same level of phobia as if the event had happened to the person who witnessed it. The bee sting, for example, could have happened to a friend. The memory is sealed regardless of who experienced the event. Perhaps no trauma had to have happened at all, but the body and brain assume trauma might accompany whatever is being feared. In the case of a blood phobia, for instance, some scientists believe that passing out at the sight of blood is a leftover ancestral brain wiring. The theory is that the body is being proactive by dropping blood pressure to very low levels—so low that the person passes out—to keep him or her from bleeding out after having been cut. Even if the person has no memory of ever bleeding, scientists think that passing out is instinctual to keep the person safe in dangerous environments.

> "If a child is not helped to understand the fear and the meaning of the worry, he may feel powerless and thus may worry more."[16]
>
> —Lynne Kenney, a pediatric psychologist

Memory Retention

The brain goes to great lengths to protect memories associated with survival. As brain health expert and neuropsychologist Dr. Paul

Social Media and Anxiety-Induced Phobia

Social media, by definition, is based on social interaction. It was created to foster a greater sense of community. And many agree that social media has increased interpersonal connections among teens, especially those geographically divided. But some studies suggest that it has had the opposite effect on teens and, in some cases, is contributing to the growth of social phobia.

The impersonal aspect of being on one's phone to keep up with social media might be preventing in-person conversation and connection. In a crowded room, teens can become isolated as they stare at phone screens instead of engaging in face-to-face conversation, which is the very core of social interaction. Having a heavy concentration of text-based and online conversations can prevent teens from learning important social cues that come from reading facial expressions and verbal intonation. "It puts everybody in a nonverbal disabled context, where body language, facial expression, and even the smallest kinds of vocal reactions are rendered invisible," says Catherine Steiner-Adair, a clinical psychologist and author of *The Big Disconnect*. When teens are unable to practice social skills, they are more anxious in group settings.

The invisibleness creates other dangers, such as sending potentially harsh messages. It all snowballs into more anxious teens sending more anxious texts, read by more anxious teens. Although social media was created to bring people together, in some instances it may actually be causing strong anxiety and fear—to the point of phobia—that prevents the very social community it was designed to create.

Nussbaum says, "There is no greater or more complicated system than the human brain!" The complex mind is divided into several parts. The medulla oblongata is the part of the brain that regulates or manages basic life functions like breathing. Located in the lower part of the brain stem, it is the part of the brain that sends signals to the heart to start beating faster when placed in fight-or-flight situations. The amygdala is the part of the brain that handles the memory of emotions, especially fear. Nussbaum explains that the amygdala region "helps with many critical skills, including memory and new learning, language comprehension, auditory processing, spatial processing, attention, spirituality [and] emotion."[17] It controls the way one handles fear and how one views and reacts to situations that might be potentially threatening or dangerous. It remembers the time when the medulla oblongata sent signals that caused the body to run to safety—or worse, the time when the signals were ignored and danger ensued. The amygdala has an extremely good memory. It is built for survival.

"There is no greater or more complicated system than the human brain!"[17]

—Paul Nussbaum, a clinical neuropsychologist

Anytime that person is in a similar situation in which that fear is triggered, whether by a sound, a smell, a taste, or something touched or seen, that memory is yanked into the forefront. The amygdala brings out the memory, and therefore the fear, to get the person ready to run or fight. The brain is trying to protect the person by reminding him or her of the danger. The goal is to get the person to safely avoid that thing (like a bee) or situation (like a tall ladder).

Memory triggers can be powerful. A person might hear the buzz of a hair dryer and think it is a bee. Or a person might be at the top of an indoor stairwell and suddenly feel as if he or she is on top of a roof. With a phobia, the brain cannot always distinguish between the real thing (a buzzing bee or rooftop) and the memory of the fear (the sound of a bee, even if it is a hair dryer, or the height of a rooftop, even if the person is indoors). The body is placed on high alert, as if the situation were real, and the fear becomes real. Panic ensues. Even when the sufferer learns there is no chance of getting stung because there is no flying insect in sight, the senses have already been activated and bodily reactions have been set into motion. It is not a conscious decision; it happens automatically. Phobic people are sent into panic mode before they even get the chance to talk themselves out of it. The all-clear brain message to turn off the fight-or-flight symptoms might not sink in for half an hour or longer. By then, the body has already been seized by fear. It takes time for the heart to stop racing, the cheeks to stop flushing, and the breathing to slow. Even if the threat is not real, the symptoms are.

Life Experiences

A person's daily life can be a contributing factor to a phobia as well. According to a study by the Department of Sociology at the University of Toronto, negative life events, such as natural disasters and life-threatening situations like war or unsafe living environments, are especially likely to play a role in the onset of a phobia. Yet two people could experience the same real-life battle-ridden situation and come out of it with completely different perspectives. One might have lifelong internal scars, but the other might be left unbothered.

One example would be families that move away from a war-torn country. Hearing loud banging noises that sound like gunfire

Growing up in the midst of war or violence can lead to phobias such as ligyrophobia, which is the fear of sharp or loud noises. Someone with this phobia might experience extreme anxiety even during a Fourth of July fireworks show.

might trigger bad memories of their past, making them uncomfortable with loud, short bursts of sound. One teen might leave the country behind and, although a little more fearful of noises than the average person, otherwise not be bothered by them. Another might have that fear grow so unmanageable that it becomes ligyrophobia, which is the fear of sharp or loud noises. Fourth of July fireworks would be a different experience for each of them.

In this example, both teens would have been exposed to the same childhood trauma. Both teens would be exposed to the same fireworks. Yet one teen might be able to enjoy the annual holiday celebration while the other would stay home, cowering in fear. Analysts are not able to pinpoint with complete accuracy what makes the same life experiences harder for some people to deal with than others. Siblings have been studied to try to determine the differences since they have virtually the same life experiences. Nonetheless, each case seems to have a myriad of different factors that contribute to one sibling developing a phobia while another does not. Science has not found an easy answer.

Genetics

It could be that DNA is a factor in who is more likely to be emotionally scarred and who is more likely to get over it. A person's biological makeup can play a role in how the brain stores memories and how the body reacts to fear. Phobia could be partly due to the genes and temperament a person inherits. Inherited genetic traits from ancestors and parents influence how the brain senses and regulates anxiety, shyness, nervousness, and stress reactions. Those born with a shy temperament tend to be cautious and sensitive in new situations and prefer the familiar. Therapists have determined that most people who develop social phobia already have a shy temperament. A child who is shy and sensitive, or is nervous and worries a lot, is more prone to have fears and phobias as he or she gets older. That is not to say that every shy person will develop a phobia. But it is more likely that a shy person will have a phobia than an outgoing person.

Stressed Out from Television?

Can watching television create anxiety? Yes. Can watching television create trauma? Yes. Can watching television create a trauma-induced phobia? Maybe. A study in the *Journal of the American Academy of Child & Adolescent Psychiatry* examined the extent to which children's television-viewing practices are associated with symptoms of psychological trauma. Several hypotheses were tested. One hypothesis assumed that children who watch greater amounts of television per day would report higher levels of trauma symptoms than children who watch less television. The study used an anonymous questionnaire to survey students in third through eighth grade in eleven Ohio public schools. Students filled out the forms on their own. The survey found that heavy television viewing by children may indicate the presence of problems such as depression and anxiety. The administrators of the survey concluded that kids who watch a lot of television have a higher tendency toward trauma symptoms like anxiety and depression and recommended that psychiatrists and other mental health professionals working with children screen them for trauma symptoms. According to the Anxiety and Depression Association of America, about half of all people diagnosed with depression are also diagnosed with an anxiety disorder, placing those young people at higher risk for developing a trauma-induced phobia.

What is unknown is whether it is truly genetic—something passed down in the DNA that causes the fear—or whether it is a learned behavior that has developed over time and as a result of life experiences. What science does know is that it is family related. The National Institutes of Health reports that 15 to 25 percent of children growing up with an agoraphobic parent, for instance, will also develop the phobia.

No so-called phobia gene has been identified, and scientists do not think one gene is responsible. Katherina K. Hauner, a postdoctoral fellow at Northwestern University's Feinberg School of Medicine, thinks acquiring a phobia is a combination of genetic and environmental factors. "Estimates of genetic contributions to specific phobia range from roughly 25 to 65 percent, although we do not know which genes have a leading part,"[18] she says. In her studies, Hauner has found variants in genes that might make it more likely someone will develop a phobia or other psychological disorders.

Dr. Edmund J. Bourne emphasizes that *both* nature and nurture play a role in the onset of phobia. In his book *The Anxiety & Phobia Workbook*, he states that one does not inherit agoraphobia, social phobia, or even panic attacks from parents. "What is inherited seems to be a *general personality type* that predisposes you to be overly anxious," Bourne says. "This is a volatile, excitable, reactive personality that is more easily set off by any slightly threatening stimulus than is the personality of individuals without anxiety disorders." He explains that whether or not teens develop social phobias can depend on the degree to which they learned to feel ashamed in situations where they were expected to perform. The development of panic attacks might depend on the nature and degree of stress to which a teen is exposed. He summarizes that heredity and life experiences are but a few of the factors playing a role in any type of anxiety disorder that may develop. "In short," say Bourne, "while heredity might cause you to be born with a more reactive, excitable nervous system, childhood experiences, conditioning, and stress all serve to shape the particular type of anxiety disorder you subsequently develop."[19] The good news is that the effect of these negative experiences can be turned around with some focused slow-but-steady effort. Just as fear can be learned, it can also be unlearned.

> "While heredity might cause you to be born with a more reactive, excitable nervous system, childhood experiences, conditioning, and stress all serve to shape the particular type of anxiety disorder you subsequently develop."[19]
>
> —Dr. Edmund J. Bourne, an anxiety treatment specialist

Risk Factors

Although the exact causes of phobias are unknown, several risk factors have been identified. Risk factors are reasons or issues that increase the odds of a person developing the phobia. These risk factors include age, family history, personality, and trauma. Having one or more risk factors does not mean one will develop a phobia. It simply means it is more likely to happen. Not knowing how or why the phobia started will not impact curing it, however. Therapists agree that the cause of a phobia has no bearing on the ability to get rid of it.

CHAPTER THREE

What Is It Like to Live with Phobias?

With phobias, thoughts and fears get exaggerated in a sufferer's mind. The person starts to focus on the bad or embarrassing things that could happen instead of the reality of what is happening. This makes a situation seem much worse than it is. The fear creates anxiety, which can worsen and deepen the fear. Fear and anxiety are two different things. Fear can be described as looking over and seeing a 350-pound (159 kg) tiger about to pounce and feeling panic, if not terror. Anxiety is feeling the discomfort without knowing or being able to pinpoint the exact cause. Both emotions result in distress.

A person with a phobia is not able to distinguish between the odds of a rare occurrence happening (low) and the likelihood of a rare event not happening (high). Instead of recognizing that it is very unlikely an emergency situation will occur when out to dinner, for example, they will think it is bound to happen.

A person with a phobia wants to avoid any chance of encountering his or her fear. To prevent and avoid potential accidents, a phobic person will choose to stay at home. By minimizing outdoor exposure, he or she feels safer. Avoiding the situation seems like a good idea, and a relief at first, but it actually makes things worse. By not facing the situation that is feared, it reinforces the fear. It convinces the person that the situation is too overwhelming and keeps him or her at home instead of facing that fear, which is an important part of recovery. Likewise, it creates other problems, including isolation, loneliness, and missed opportunities.

Fear, Avoidance, and Anxiety

Emily Ford was a teen afflicted with severe social anxiety. In her book *What You Must Think of Me: A Firsthand Account of One Teenager's Experience with Social Anxiety Disorder*, she explains her initial difficulty in publicly admitting her fears. At first she was not sure she had a problem that warranted help. She thought that perhaps she was just experiencing typical nerves about school and making friends. She started to become very self-conscious about what she said in class, about the clothes she wore, and about the people with whom she spoke. She felt as if she kept making mistakes and was being judged. She thought it must be obvious to everyone else that she did not fit in and that people must be talking about her behind her back. When she realized she was becoming more socially awkward—a realization that only made her feel worse and, in turn, behave more awkwardly—she knew she needed help.

But even as she was getting treatment, she was not sure she would be taken seriously by others. That made her want to avoid others all the more. "In a society consumed with syndromes, disorders, and pharmaceutical advertisements, I assumed it appeared as though I'd hopped on the 'we're all disordered' bandwagon, hiding a personality flaw behind the more sophisticated and increasingly popular term *anxiety*," Ford says. "Still, *I* knew social anxiety disorder was a real condition substantially different from shyness. It had very real symptoms and very real consequences."[20] Her fears of what other people would think about her anxiety kept her from seeking help sooner. She wishes they had not. But that is typical with social phobia.

Ford's average weekday probably started like that of most teens with social phobia: she would wake up an emotional wreck, with her stomach tied in knots, and hope to talk her parents into letting her skip a day of school. When it was clear that she would have to attend classes, she would brush her teeth, get her things ready, and resign herself to another day of inner torture. She would torment herself with thoughts like, "At least, please don't let this be the day when everyone finds out that I'm crazy."[21]

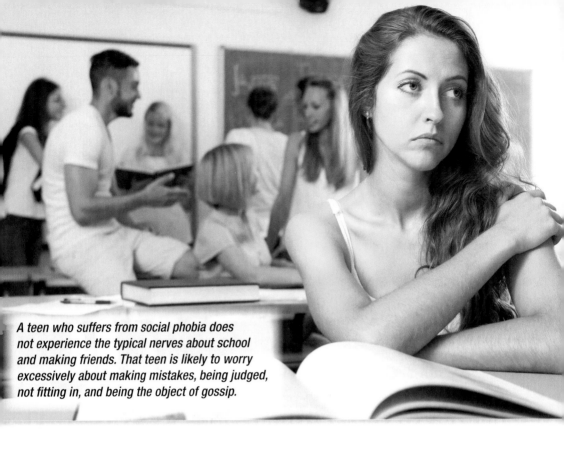

A teen who suffers from social phobia does not experience the typical nerves about school and making friends. That teen is likely to worry excessively about making mistakes, being judged, not fitting in, and being the object of gossip.

When a friendly classmate would smile and greet her, Ford assumed it was really condescending pity. When teachers gave class instructions on writing neater and taking more time with homework, Ford assumed it was a personal attack on *her* disguised as general comments. It ate away at her self-esteem. "I spent each day of my high school believing deep down that my teachers hated me. I thought that at every moment people were making fun of me and whispering nasty comments underneath their breath,"[22] Ford says.

There was no safe haven for Ford at school. Everywhere she looked, she found scrutinizing eyes and unwelcoming stares. Teens like Ford who suffer from social phobia dread common areas like the lunchroom. They constantly worry about where to sit or with whom to eat. Ford, like other social phobia sufferers, would question whether a tablemate's cough was just a cough or really meant "Don't sit there." Did that raised eyebrow mean "We don't want you here"? A person suffering from social phobia would never have enough nerve to ask.

The worst part is that these types of worries happen on a daily basis. Left unchecked, the person suffers day in and day out. Typically, an outsider would simply see a shy, quiet teen. Externally there may be no signs of pain, but the individual constantly suffers on the inside.

Missing Out on Life

Social phobia can take a toll on the outside too. Staying cooped up at home, spending all that time away from others, is not without cost. One of the major effects teens encounter with isolation is lost friendships. Although it is possible to maintain some friends, most friendships become awkward when the ailing teen is unable to effectively communicate. Close friends tend to drift away. Even though the anxiety-ridden teen often chooses and prefers to be alone in order to prevent any potentially embarrassing situations, solitude eventually causes emotional damage.

> "I spent each day of my high school believing deep down that my teachers hated me. I thought that at every moment people were making fun of me and whispering nasty comments underneath their breath."[22]
>
> —Teen social phobia sufferer Emily Ford

Social phobia also prevents teens from getting the most out of school. It can keep them from giving a demonstration, reading aloud, or participating in the classroom. A teen with social phobia might be too nervous to ask a question in class or go to a teacher for help. Social phobia may ultimately keep them behind in schoolwork and negatively affect their grades.

In the bigger picture, those who suffer from social phobia are missing out on life. Social phobia prevents sufferers from meeting new people and trying new things. It can keep someone from auditioning for the school play, being in a talent show, going to a basketball game with friends, volunteering with a charity, trying out for a team, or joining a club. It also prevents them from making the normal, everyday mistakes that help people learn and grow.

Teens undergoing treatment for social phobia repeatedly say they wish they had sought out treatment as soon as they had figured out something was wrong. "It would have saved years of struggle, depression, and isolation," Ford says. "Those are not scars I wear proudly; they're the result of fearing what someone might think if I were to speak up and ask for help. *The bravest thing I've ever done* was to reach out and actively seek the assistance I desperately wanted and knew that I needed."[23]

The Fear of Flying

Not every phobia is all-consuming. Some phobias, mainly specific phobias like the fear of pigs or the fear of knives, come into play only when the person comes into contact with the feared item or subject. Daily life can be somewhat normal when fear is absent. As soon as the person has contact with the feared item or subject, however, the trouble begins and panic starts.

The fear of flying is called aviophobia. One might assume that people with aviophobia have suffered some sort of trauma in their past related to flying. Maybe they were in a plane crash or they survived a cockpit fire. But it is also possible that they have never even been in or near a plane. A phobia does not always result from a specific event. A teen with a specific phobia might be living an otherwise normal life, without a hint that a phobia is around the corner, when suddenly it hits.

John DiScala had no signs of trouble and no history of travel woes. When he was sixteen, his doctor diagnosed him with asthma. At the time, the doctor told him he might have a problem breathing on a plane because the cabin is pressurized. DiScala did not give the doctor's comments much thought; he went on with his life. A year later, however, he and his parents were at a New York airport waiting to board a flight to Australia when suddenly terror struck. "I felt this tingling all over my body," DiScala says. "I felt like I was not in control."[24] DiScala remembered the doctor saying he might have trouble breathing on an airplane. He could not stop thinking about it. The thought grew and grew. He refused to get on the

> "I felt this tingling all over my body. I felt like I was not in control."[24]
>
> —John DiScala, aviophobe

42

A person who has a fear of flying might lead a perfectly normal life until he or she is confronted with the prospect of flying. This phobia results in a paralyzing fear of air travel, a fear that is not rational or even related to the safety of flying.

plane and never boarded the flight to visit his sisters. His fear did not go away once he left the airport either. It got worse. He grew so afraid of flying that he refused to travel again for more than three years. In DiScala's case, aviophobia was based on the fear of having an asthma attack on the plane and not being able to breathe. Others with the fear of flying might have claustrophobia or a fear of heights; still others might dislike the lack of control, not trust technology, or simply fear that the plane will crash.

Helping Others

Not many kids pull a knife on their mom to get out of going to school. But that is just what Summer Garcia did when she was eleven. She would try anything to get out of going, from shouting and swearing to kicking her mother. "It was strange because I really wanted to go to school. I felt abnormal and like I was missing out. I wanted to be there but I just couldn't do it," Summer says.

She was not bullied and had friends she wanted to be with, but she also had an intense fear blocking her. Once she got to school she was fine. The fear did not exist in any other part of her life, only in school. It was not until age fourteen that a psychologist diagnosed her with school phobia, or didaskaleinophobia.

To prevent other kids from having to go through the terrible ordeal, Summer started an outreach program on an international website called Fixers. She has a team of twenty-one people helping her get the word out. They have created and posted a video about the disorder, and Summer has been talking about the condition in newspapers and on television. "For our . . . campaign, my group and I want to show that school phobia is a real anxiety disorder and should be taken seriously. Hopefully this will raise enough awareness and help others like me get the support they need."

Quoted in Sarah Jones, "School Phobia: Just Setting Foot in the Classroom Filled My Daughter with Terror," *Daily Express,* May 12, 2014. www.express.co.uk.

"Summer," Profile. www.fixers.org.uk.

Consumed by Fear

Most aviophobes will say how badly they *want* to fly but simply *cannot*. Statistics, numbers, and facts—such as the fact that commercial pilots have more than three thousand hours of flight-time experience—do not necessarily calm the nerves of an aviophobe. A paralyzing fear of air travel is not usually rational. "It doesn't have to do with how safe flying is," says Tom Bunn, a psychologist and the founder of a program to help ease the fear of flying. "Panic is eventually just one bump, noise, or frightening thought away."[25]

It can help to calm the nerves if the fear can be predicted. But those fears are not always consistent and do not always kick in like DiScala's did, when he arrived at the airport. The fear of flying may only appear upon landing. It might only kick in if there is midair turbulence. Gasping for breath and having sweaty palms and butterflies in the stomach could start at the mere mention of a trip, or they may start the week leading up to the flight—that is, if the sufferer is even willing to attempt getting on a plane. Some teens will not even consider driving by the airport, let alone walking to the gate.

Those who can and do manage to get on the plane are consumed with constant fear during the trip. They are hypersensitive to every aspect of the flight, from the tone of voice of the pilot on the intercom to the way the plane handles normal turbulence. As Robert Bor, a psychologist, pilot, and coauthor of *Overcome Your Fear of Flying*, explains, "In people's minds they've built up a story of what's going to go wrong, and then they look for cues to validate their story. So if they see a flight attendant looking a bit serious, they will take a cue from that that the plane is in trouble." The scared traveler is on the constant lookout for any sort of threat and sees hazards where none exists. When traveling with a patient on a healing flight, taken to get the patient more comfortable being in the air, Bor says the patient kept nervously looking up at the flight attendants. "In her mind, because they were walking quickly, it meant they were gathering together emergency procedures and briefing one another about the disaster that was about to happen."[26] No catastrophe happened. The patient spent the entire flight seeing trouble that did not exist.

> "Panic is eventually just one bump, noise, or frightening thought away."[25]
>
> —Psychologist Tom Bunn

Moving On

Although aviophobes are in terror around travel time and while in the air, they are not necessarily consumed with fear on a day-to-day basis. They do not wake up thinking about it, have trouble eating, or lose sleep fretting over it. Typically, the fear comes into play only when sufferers consider flying. Talking about flying can upset them and get them thinking about their fear, but most sufferers do not have major symptoms or physical issues on a daily basis.

Nonetheless, aviophobia still takes a toll. Without intervention, fearful flyers miss out on all kinds of life events. Any event that requires more than a trip by car, boat, or train is out of the question. International travel, trips to see faraway grandparents over school break, and sports tournaments in distant cities are some of the things aviophobes miss out on.

Luckily, a version of long-term recovery is possible for those afraid of flying. In fact, DiScala not only got over his fear of flying but also thrives on air travel now. In his case, his desire to travel was greater than his fear, so he got help. DiScala now helps others with the fear of flying and writes a travel blog centered around flying the globe. Any minor setbacks that he may have are overridden with the end thought: travel is worth it. The fear may still exist in some lesser form, but it is not preventing him from getting the most out of life. On a long-term basis, most aviophobes can be cured. The same is true for most specific types of phobias.

Agoraphobia Is Hard on Teens

Agoraphobia is rare. According to the *Diagnostic and Statistical Manual of Mental Disorders*, fewer than 1 percent of Americans have been diagnosed with the phobia. Yet Dr. Mark Eisenstadt, author of *Freedom from Agoraphobia,* believes the disorder is underreported. He thinks 5 percent of the population, as many as one in twenty people, could be suffering silently from agoraphobia. Women are two to three times more likely to have the phobia than men, and it is more common in teenagers and young adults. At least half of these young people are suffering from depression as well.

Teens living with agoraphobia may have it worse than any other phobia sufferer. Agoraphobia is like having many phobias rolled into one. Studies have found that agoraphobes are afraid of having a panic attack in an open space. Like those who suffer from social phobia, they are afraid of being unable to find shelter, run for or find help, or keep their panic attack hidden from others while in the open. Agoraphobes therefore often have underlying social phobia. They may also suffer from specific fears, such as the fear of bats, the fear of blood, and others. All of these fears add up to one larger fear of leaving the comfort of home.

One teen explains her pain this way: "I've had anxiety my whole life, but it never affected me quite like acute agoraphobia. . . . It came on almost overnight, and suddenly I couldn't leave the house without feeling sick. It got to the point that even *imagining* leaving the house got me feeling sick to my stomach, like I

Teens who suffer from agoraphobia experience distress in crowded places such as at concerts, in shopping malls, and on subways. Agoraphobics are afraid of having a panic attack where others can see them.

Panic Attacks

When most people think of a panic attack, they envision someone gasping for breath, maybe needing to sit down and take a shot of an inhaler. But there is more going on. Panic attacks cause feelings of intense fear that are accompanied by a pounding heart; sweating; trembling; shaking hands and knees; problems swallowing; hot or cold feelings; nausea; hyperventilating, which causes dizziness and problems breathing; chest pain, as if having a heart attack; and/or a strong fear of dying. Typically these symptoms occur all at once. Sufferers have described panic attacks as a feeling of being chased by dinosaurs and wanting to run like mad but feeling frozen in place. Some describe the feeling of ice racing through their veins. Others say they feel like they are on fire, walls are quickly closing in on them, or a train has rolled onto their chest. Many feel like they are suffocating and cannot call out for help.

Panics attacks can last from twenty minutes to an hour. Upon recovery, the sufferer can still feel shaky, get sick, suffer from diarrhea, feel faint, and have breathing problems. Some have said they feel relieved when the attack is over, as if the buildup of pressure has been released.

was going to throw up or pass out or something. I kept skipping school and staying home." She ended up seeking help from a school psychologist, who suggested she go to group therapy for anxiety. Therapy helped, but it was not enough; the teen then talked to her doctor, who put her on anxiety medication. "It helped immensely,"[27] she says.

With agoraphobia, teens are uncomfortable taking public transportation, especially alone. They feel distress in crowds at concerts or standing in line. Outdoors, they are uncomfortable in large, open spaces such as parking lots or fields. Smaller, closed-in spaces, such as stores, movie theaters, and elevators, are also regularly avoided. Ben describes his fears this way: "I was terrified to leave the house. I wouldn't ride on planes, trains or any form of public transport. I was terrified of being caught in traffic jams, lifts [elevators], shopping centres, open spaces, crowds and especially hot, crowded rooms." He also had social phobia. "I always felt judged. Public speaking was unthinkable. . . . I was terrified of being away from home. . . . I also knew that if I left the house, that I would be stricken with fear."[28] Ben took up meditation and running, changed his mindset, and went on medication for five years to help ease his agoraphobia. He now flies on airplanes, happily chats with new people, and enjoys wide open spaces. He considers himself cured, with the exception of public speaking.

Taking It Slow

Without intervention or treatment, agoraphobes might be able to handle some outdoor trips without attack or impact. They might feel comfortable going to a handful of familiar places, such as a friend's house or a restaurant they have been to time and time again. They might be able to handle the outdoors under certain situations, such as during the day or with a limited-size crowd that is not too noisy.

Then again, even familiar places may have trouble spots. Emma was fifteen when her agoraphobia started. She was able to attend school but could not handle big halls with hundreds of people, especially when it came time to take tests. She was able to get special permission to take final exams in a separate room. Once that change was made, she performed well enough to go on to college.

Other teens deal with their agoraphobia by learning to identify a so-called safe person. The phobic teen feels comfortable with that safe person, likely a parent or close friend, who is able to help coax the sufferer to travel a little farther away from home, stay out a little longer than the last time, or try out a new, less familiar location.

It is much more common for teen agoraphobes to find any excuse to avoid the outside world, though. They stay at home and avoid reasons to be away from the comfort of home, missing out on sports, dances, charitable events, and after-school activities. They want to participate but cannot muster the courage to leave

49

their house. They often regret staying home, and depression is a common side effect.

A phobia sufferer's symptoms will depend on what he or she fears, how intense the fear is, and what is taking place in the person's surroundings. Regardless of the phobia, feelings of panic and dread are often present, as is the physical and emotional misery that comes with them. After a phobic episode, it is common for the person to feel embarrassed and depressed, which leads to further negative feelings about the episode. Luckily, help is available.

CHAPTER FOUR

Can Phobias Be Treated or Cured?

Most teens who suffer from psychiatric disorders never receive any treatment for the disorder, according to a Duke University study. Teens are self-conscious, embarrassed, or ashamed by their phobias and are afraid to talk about them. That is unfortunate because people with phobias can learn to manage fear, develop confidence and coping skills, and stop avoiding things that make them anxious. Although the understanding of how and why phobias exist remains limited, science has made great strides in remedying them. "No, you cannot make your fears vanish with the wave of a magic wand. But . . . you can build your courage muscles," encourages life coach Debra Smouse. "How? By taking small steps. By tackling your fear in increments. By making a commitment to yourself."[29] Smouse has found that her clients start getting results as soon as they simply acknowledge their fears.

If teens get help early on, a phobia is less likely to last through adulthood. At a minimum, getting help at the beginning or early stages of a phobia can soften its effects. "Early intervention is always a positive," says therapist Nancy Milla. "If a teen learns coping skills, they are more prepared to manage the symptoms of the phobia, thus lessening the severity if it continues into adulthood."[30]

> "If a teen learns coping skills, they are more prepared to manage the symptoms of the phobia, thus lessening the severity if it continues into adulthood."[30]
>
> —Nancy Milla, a licensed marriage and family therapist

Treatment depends on the type of phobia. Social phobias are usually treated with therapy and/or medication. Specific phobias can typically be managed with various forms of therapy. Agoraphobia, especially when accompanied by a panic disorder, is usually treated with more intensive therapy and/or medication.

Support systems are also important. Having help and reassurance from a few key people can greatly boost the healing process. With the support of friends and family, for example, a sufferer can garner the confidence to step out of his or her comfort zone a little easier, if not faster, than going it alone. Treatment and assistance in school are also helpful. Without the backup and agreement of school officials to help, treatment will take longer and be less effective. Encouragement and positive reinforcement of goals being met is a great incentive for a phobia sufferer to continue treatment.

Counseling

Counseling can help young people with phobias and everyone around them. Therapists are quick to point out that the fear, anxiety, and other symptoms are caused by a disorder with complex genetic and environmental origins, not by a flawed person or a bad attitude. Sometimes hearing "It's not your fault" can have amazing healing properties in itself. Whether counseling is done individually, with family, or in a group setting, it can reduce the negative impact on daily life and ideally lead to long-term healing. A variety of psychological interventions are used, depending on the phobia.

Individual psychotherapy involves meeting with a therapist one-on-one. It is generally the first line of treatment for teens with anxiety-driven phobias like social phobia and agoraphobia. Individual psychotherapy can help young people become aware of and address self-image issues.

Exposure therapy is widely accepted as the most effective treatment for anxieties and phobias, and it is an excellent choice for specific phobias. During exposure therapy, the person faces his or her fear little by little, getting bolder each time. A teen

A therapist listens to her patient describe her fears and concerns. Counseling can help increase self-confidence and provide tools for reducing the effects of phobias on daily life.

afraid of spiders, for example, might start by looking at a picture of a spider. The time gets extended from a peek to a glance to a several-second-long look. Slowly the person afraid of the arachnid would work up the courage to touch the photo. The next steps would involve being in the same room with a spider and then working one's way up to touching a spider. Studies show that the vast majority of patients complete treatment within ten sessions.

Cognitive behavior therapy (CBT) can teach social phobia sufferers new skills to help reduce anxiety when interacting with others. In CBT, teens discuss the negative thoughts, feelings, and reactions associated with their phobia. A trained clinician then guides them to think of new, different, and more positive (alternative) reactions. They are then given a chance to practice

and master new thoughts, feelings, and reactions outside the clinical visit. CBT replaces old, unhealthy thoughts and reactions with new, healthier ones. This is most helpful if teens can place themselves where the phobia can be encountered often, such as around heights or dogs. CBT has been especially effective with social phobia and agoraphobia.

Family physician Jeffrey Hill has worked one-on-one with phobic teens. "Most teens that I see . . . need guided help. Their fears were learned. I help them unlearn them," Hill says. "Basically, to be most effective, they need to experience what they are afraid of, little by little, I mean really experience it, and see that nothing bad happens. It's a minimalistic approach. It's simple, really. But it works."[31]

There are several other therapy options. Family therapy can be very helpful when issues are affecting the family as a whole. It helps the family learn ways to support the teen who is going through the tough time. Group therapy, in which a bunch of other teens suffering from the same disorder gather together for help, is another option. Both are ways to talk openly and freely about the impact of the disorder, without judgment or fear of being misunderstood. It can be helpful to know one is not alone in one's suffering and feelings. Understandably, those with social phobia are uncomfortable meeting new people and speaking in front of others, so they shy away from group sessions. But both family and group therapy have been found to be very effective for anxious teens and their families.

Rewarding the process itself can be helpful too. In her book *Freeing Your Child from Anxiety,* Dr. Tamar E. Chansky recommends using "tangible reinforcers and rewards" toward taking baby steps in overcoming phobias. She believes that rewards are great motivators, and the rewards do not have to be big or expensive. Chansky explains that positive rewards "change the tone of the work from serious and fearful to something positive—working toward getting pancakes for breakfast, scoring a free pass from taking out the trash, or having the privilege of borrowing the car."[32]

Getting Help at School

Getting help from school, referred to as school-based counseling, is another important piece of the treatment puzzle. This is not the same as therapy sessions occurring in the school or during school hours. School-based counseling includes parents, caregivers, and medical professionals getting official buy-in from the school staff and administration in order for the student to get formal assistance navigating the social, behavioral, and academic demands of daily school life. Alerting a teacher that a social phobic student has a medical condition that makes it difficult for him or her to be called on in class can make the difference in how a teacher treats a student. It can greatly help how the teacher approaches the student inside as well as outside the classroom.

There are many ways that school-based counseling can help, depending on the phobia. For an agoraphobe, it might mean an

Natural Supplements: A Healthy Choice?

Are herbal treatments a good idea to help teen anxiety? Most studies are limited, and results are mixed. Experts like Dr. Daniel K. Hall-Flavin from the Mayo Clinic agree that more research is needed to understand the risks and benefits.

Chamomile, lavender, passionflower, and lemon balm are considered generally safe and somewhat effective. They have been shown to reduce some symptoms of anxiety, including nervousness and excitability. Nonetheless, chamomile can result in allergic reactions in people who are sensitive to the family of plants that includes ragweed. Likewise, oral lavender can cause constipation, headaches, nausea, and vomiting. And passionflower can cause depression when taken in large doses.

Two herbal remedies that have been repeatedly flagged for potentially danger-ous side effects are ginkgo and kava. Ginkgo seems to help by improving blood circulation, which might help the brain function better. But ginkgo seeds contain a toxin that can cause side effects like seizures and loss of consciousness. Kava, although reported to be possibly effective, has been linked to serious liver damage and even death; it is banned in several European countries. Dr. Hall-Flavin advises,

> If you're considering taking any herbal supplement as a treatment for anxiety, talk to your doctor first, especially if you take other medications. The interac-tion of some herbal supplements and certain medications can cause serious side effects. If your anxiety is interfering with daily activities, talk with your doctor. More serious forms of anxiety generally need medical treatment or psychological counseling (psychotherapy) for symptoms to improve.

Daniel K. Hall-Flavin, "Is There an Effective Herbal Treatment for Anxiety?," Mayo Clinic. www.mayoclinic.org.

approved late check-in, a designated quiet room for taking tests, an area set aside for eating lunch, or an assigned buddy for sup-port. Working together, parents, teachers, and administrators can figure out the best way to help the student thrive.

Some professionals are urging more schools to offer coun-seling services for mental health issues, including anxiety-related disorders like phobias. Among elementary and middle school students who received mental health services, the *Journal of the American Academy of Child & Adolescent Psychiatry* reports that one in every eight children had some form of anxiety. Professional clinical counselor supervisor Christina Baker notes that "anxiety in young children is often manifested in behaviors such as fidgeting, distraction, poor concentration and irritability."[33] According to Baker, school-based counseling is key to helping kids get the right treatment they need, as early as the student needs it. With the National Institutes of Health reporting that anxiety-related disorders are most common at the high school level, Baker feels it is critical that youth have more services available. She agrees that educators and administrators can be critical to a student's success in treatment.

Emotional Support Animals

A different technique that might be helpful for phobic teens is the use of emotional support animals. One Texas teen found assistance in the form of a small dog. Aliana Hunt was fifteen when she realized she needed help. Her mom took her to their family pediatrician for her social anxiety, which was turning into a phobia. Her social fear was causing her to lose friends, preventing her from making new ones, negatively affecting her grades, and overall causing constant anguish. "I wanted to get her whatever help she needed and whatever was available to her,"[34] her mom, Emily, says. After listening to what was going on, the pediatrician immediately prescribed antidepressants, which are commonly used to treat anxiety. Although not a fan of medicinal intervention in general, Aliana was not the least bit reluctant to follow the doctor's orders. "I didn't hesitate to start taking the prescription. I mean, my mom and I looked into what the drugs were, what they were going to do to me, what the side effects might cause, and all that. It's not like I took it lightly," she says. "But I went to the doctor for help. I needed help. I knew I needed to take a drastic step."[35]

> "I went to the doctor for help. I needed help. I knew I needed to take a drastic step."[35]
>
> —Aliana Hunt, a teen social phobia sufferer

The pediatrician was the first of many steps the Hunt family took. Ultimately the family consulted a psychiatrist to continue the monitoring of the antidepressant/anxiety meds. Aliana's mom also did some research about how animals can help with anxiety and calm kids during an episode. Eventually they family adopted a small dog named Oliver. Aliana takes the dog with her everywhere: to grocery stores, movie theaters, family outings, and, on occasion (with permission), even to school. The dog serves as ongoing emotional support for the teen. It also offers opportunities for Aliana to engage in social interaction, which is something she has had difficulties with and wanted help working on. Strangers will often come up to her and ask if they can pet her dog, what his name is, and what kind of dog he is. This serves as a chance for the shy teen to actively participate in conversations.

Emotional support animals are not recognized the same as a service animal, meaning they do not have a national registry. But emotional support animals can be prescribed by a licensed psychologist or medical doctor, much as a medication would be prescribed. Aliana is careful not to take Oliver where he might not be welcome. To be called out on it would almost certainly cause her anxiety to spike. Overall, the emotional support dog, as well as the medication, has been a lifesaver for Aliana. "Oliver calms me down in social situations and is a conversation starter," Aliana says. "He has helped me so much that I now work as a hostess at a local restaurant, something that two years ago would never have been possible. In Texas, Friday night football games are a huge deal, and when I know Oliver will be with me, it's easy to want to go."[36] Emily Hunt is thankful the family found the right solution: "I didn't know if the combination of medication and animal therapy would work out, but seeing her now, I know it was the right choice."[37]

> "I didn't know if the combination of medication and animal therapy would work out, but seeing her now, I know it was the right choice."[37]
>
> —Emily Hunt, the mother of a teen with social phobia

Emotional support animals have benefited some young people with phobias. An emotional support dog, for instance, can help bring calm during a phobic episode and can also help the teen learn to engage with other people.

Medication

Medical intervention at some level is almost always required, whether in the form of medication or the help of a therapist, family doctor, or psychologist. Counselors of any degree play a vital role in helping teens overcome their issues and phobias. Initially, a therapist can help teens recognize the physical sensations caused by the fight-or-flight response and teach them to interpret and handle these initial panic signs more accurately. When therapy alone is not enough, customized medical assistance may be warranted. Medical professionals create an overall plan for healing, helping build skills and confidence along the way. They may prescribe a variety of medications, as needed.

No medicines yet exist to cure phobias. The US Food and Drug Administration (FDA) has not approved any specific medication to treat phobias in teens, but medications approved for other uses and age groups can be prescribed for young people with phobias. Antidepressants are commonly used and have been found effective. The medication eases anxiety, which makes the social phobia easier to overcome. The FDA allows medical professionals to use their best judgment when prescribing medication for conditions for which the medication has not been specifically approved. Medications all work in much same way: they treat or ease the physical symptoms that accompany panic attacks and phobic episodes but not the phobia itself.

The drugs used for phobias suppress the output of neurotransmitters that interpret fear. The drugs help stop or prevent the pounding heart, racing thoughts, prickly scalp, and hyperventilation associated with extreme anxiety. The drugs treat the symptoms—not the phobia. The reason they work well is that the person taking the medication has fewer or less severe reactions to that which upsets him or her. The person without the fear reaction can more easily overcome the phobia. A teen afraid to walk in the backyard because he fears being stung by a bee, for example, might be prescribed antianxiety medication. The medication will prevent him from having a panic attack when the sliding glass door to the backyard opens. It might allow him to feel comfortable enough to sit in the backyard without fear of a bee buzzing by. Without the inner turmoil and physical reactions, he can have the confidence to walk by a rose bush on his way to a bench.

Selective serotonin reuptake inhibitors (SSRIs) like Prozac and Lexapro are one of the most commonly used types of antidepressant medications prescribed for anxiety and are often a psychiatrist's first choice. SSRIs have been proven to be very effective for anxiety, are nonaddictive, do not cause memory impairment or interfere with psychotherapy, and have minimal side effects. Other often-prescribed medications include serotonin norepinephrine reuptake inhibitors (SNRIs) like Effexor and Cymbalta and a class called azapirone that includes generic buspirone. Both types are similar to SSRIs and have similar, low chances of side effects. They are also widely used for anxiety and phobia. These medications take about four to six weeks of daily use before reaching their maximum effectiveness. The medications have to be taken

A Virtual Reality

What do the fear of flying, the fear of heights, claustrophobia, the fear of driving, the fear of thunderstorms, arachnophobia, the fear of public speaking, agoraphobia, and social phobia all have in common? They can all be helped—if not cured—virtually. The interactive computer-generated world of virtual reality has been proven successful in treating phobias and other anxiety-related conditions. In places like the Virtual Reality Medical Center in California, modern, evidence-based, practice-friendly treatments are ridding many teens of lagging fears.

Initially, clients are connected noninvasively to a machine. Visual feedback is used to help them understand when they are relaxed and when they are anxious. The first goal for clients with phobias is to learn to recreate relaxed feelings on their own, in real-life phobic situations. Once anxiety management skills have been mastered, clients use a head-mounted virtual reality display. The virtual reality places them in an environment where they encounter their fear, whether it is a thunderstorm or driving a car. Virtual reality allows them to slowly practice these skills in exact (virtual) situations where they have felt their unwelcomed anxiety, allowing newly learned skills to be used more easily in real-world settings. In careful, controlled stages, teens are exposed to higher levels of anxiety. If anxiety becomes overwhelming, the client can return to a less stressful level or simply remove the head-mounted display and exit the virtual world. Every session is monitored by a health professional. Reported success rates at the Virtual Reality Medical Center are over 90 percent.

regularly, possibly long-term, and can have uncomfortable withdrawal symptoms if they are stopped suddenly.

Benzodiazepines like Xanax and Valium are another form of antianxiety drug. They work almost instantly, without the weeks of ramp-up required by SSRIs and SNRIs. Stephen Stahl, a psychiatrist and the chairman of the Neuroscience Education Institute, says their effectiveness on anxiety is profound. But benzodiazepines are not without problems. They cause a slowing down of thought processes and a decrease in the body's ability to move, affecting coordination and movement. Some studies show that benzodiazepines impact a person's memory and ability to learn.

And they are addictive. The federal Substance Abuse and Mental Health Services Administration reports that rehab visits involving benzodiazepine use tripled between 1998 and 2008. Given the addictive tendencies of these drugs, teens need to carefully weigh whether they should take these drugs. An open discussion with the prescribing medical professional is recommended.

Other potentially helpful medications commonly prescribed for phobias include antihistamines and medication used for nerve pain and seizures. These drugs are found to have calming effects on the brain and therefore on the nervous system, which is important when panic attacks strike. In slowing the automated fight-or-flight response time, they prevent the phobic brain from overreacting.

> "Understand that drugs will not cure you. . . . They can provide the short-term relief you need as you seek therapy or other means of healing yourself. Ultimately, drugs only mask your symptoms, they don't make anything go away indefinitely."[38]
>
> —Paul Dooley, a licensed therapist and the author of *How to Stop Anxious Thinking*

Medications might be prescribed for a short period or for long-term use. The specific medication chosen by a health care professional will depend on a number of factors, including the frequency and severity of symptoms, the patient's medical history, possible side effects, and other plans in place, such as family therapy. It might take a few tries to find the right medication that works. But as licensed therapist Paul Dooley cautions, "Understand that drugs will not cure you. Sometimes we all have difficult moments and hope for a miracle; but this is not what drugs are. They can provide the short-term relief you need as you seek therapy or other means of healing yourself. Ultimately, drugs only mask your symptoms, they don't make anything go away indefinitely."[38]

Medication Caution

Although medications can be effective in treating some phobias, doctors can be hesitant to prescribe them for all phobias. Aviophobia, for example, is one phobia for which medication is ill-advised. Antianxiety medication to reduce flight anxiety actually backfires. The main reason is that the aviophobe is in a panic mode—and, therefore, in possible need of medication—only around the time of the plane ride. Short-term benzodiazepines, which work quickly to calm the nerves for a single flight, are different than the daily anxiety medications (SSRIs or SNRIs) that someone under a doctor's care for another phobia would take. According to research at the Stanford University School of Medicine, although the person taking the short-term antianxiety medication may feel more relaxed, his or her nerves are still on high alert. Benzodiazepines may initially ease nerves, but they increase the anxious flier's sensitivity to the plane's noises and motions. Although benzodiazepines like Valium can help ease nerves for that one flight, they prevent anxious fliers from getting used to flying and prevent healing in the long run. As psychiatrist Richard A. Friedman writes,

> If you think you can outsmart your [flying] phobia with anti-anxiety medications, forget about it; they might numb you during an acute panic attack, but they will not erase your phobia. In fact, they could get in the way of therapy because they impede new learning, which is the essence of curing phobias. To kick a travel phobia, you have to fight fire with fire; you have to tolerate some anxiety to get rid of it. No shortcuts.[39]

Friedman's advice is to stick with counseling and avoid the preflight numbing effects of short-term anxiety medication.

Monitoring the Risks

There are many ways medical intervention can help treat phobias and the resulting symptoms. The majority of medications prescribed for anxiety can take up to twelve weeks before becoming effective. Many can cause side effects. Although rare, the FDA has reports of symptoms and conditions worsening with medication.

Questions have arisen about whether antidepressants can cause some teens to have suicidal thoughts. However, evidence shows that antidepressants, when carefully monitored, have safely helped many children and adolescents. Overall, medications continue to be prescribed because doctors find that the benefits outweigh the risks. Any and all medical decisions should be taken seriously and risks and benefits discussed in detail with the prescribing doctor.

Careful monitoring is recommended—and important—for any young person receiving medication. Though most side effects occur soon after starting a medicine, adverse reactions can occur weeks or even months later. A new or heightened agitation, restlessness, increased irritability, or comments about self-harm should be addressed immediately with a health professional if the symptoms sprout up at any point after the teen starts taking an antidepressant, even if it has been months. Frequent medical follow-up appointments, starting weekly for the first month, are advocated by the FDA for young people starting an antidepressant.

Finding a Balance

Therapy and medication can work either alone or together. Many professionals view therapy as having the edge over medication, though. They believe that the benefits of counseling tend to last well beyond the end of treatment. Patients can use the skills and behaviors they learned in therapy long after the counselor-led sessions have ended. Recovery achieved in therapy occurs from learning. The brain can be rewired to stop fearing a thing, event, situation, or person. Therapy has been shown to be as effective as medication, and it is most often considered to be first-line treatment for phobia. When anxiety is treated solely by medication, recovery often depends on the continued use of that medication. Side effects have to be taken into consideration and cannot be worse than then phobia itself. In many cases, the best results are when a therapy and medication plan is created by a professional, based on the specific needs of the patient. As the needs of the patient grow and change, the plan should change too.

SOURCE NOTES

Introduction: Real Fear, Real Problem

1. Mayo Clinic, "Diseases and Conditions: Phobias." www.mayoclinic.org.
2. Andrea Umbach, *Conquer Your Fears and Phobias for Teens: How to Build Courage and Stop Fear from Holding You Back*. Oakland, CA: Instant Help, 2015.
3. Quoted in Varia Fedko-Blake, "Are You Terrified of Butterflies Too!? Weird Celebrity Phobias That Will Shock You!," Movie Pilot, February 5, 2015. http://moviepilot.com.
4. Quoted in Fredric Neuman, "Overcoming Phobias: 6 Important Principles," *Fighting Fear* (blog), *Psychology Today*, June 27, 2012. www.psychologytoday.com.

Chapter One: What Are Phobias?

5. Quoted in "Childhood Fears and Anxieties," *Harvard Medical School Mental Health Letter*, August 1988. www.accg.net.
6. Quoted in Rick Nauret, "Most Teen Mental Health Problems Go Untreated," PsychCentral, November 19, 2013. http://psychcentral.com.
7. Quoted in Goodreads, "Popular Quotes." www.goodreads.com.
8. Nancy Milla, interview with the author, July 14, 2016.
9. ItsJustMe, "I'm Afraid of Normal Teenager Things, Really Hurting My Social Life," PsychCentral, November 3, 2012. http://answers.pyschcentral.com.
10. Brianna Morley, "Growing Up and the Realization of Having Emetophobia," *Life as a Teen Who Has Emetophobia* (blog), January 28, 2012. http://emetophobia-struggler.blogspot.com.

11. Quoted in Maura Judkis, "Want to Charge Your Phone at the Bar? You May Have to Pay, One Way or Another," *Washington Post*, March 8, 2016. www.washingtonpost.com.
12. K.E. Nave, "No Fear: Agoraphobia," Stage of Life: High School, March 23, 2013. www.stageoflife.com.
13. Nave, "No Fear."

Chapter Two: What Causes Phobias?

14. Quoted in Brigit Katz, "How to Avoid Passing Anxiety on to Your Kids," Child Mind Institute. http://childmind.org.
15. Quoted in Morgen E. Peck, "Harsh, Critical Parenting May Lead to Anxiety Disorder Symptoms," *Scientific American,* May 1, 2015. www.scientificamerican.com.
16. Lynne Kenney, "3 Ways to Help Children with Fears, Worries, or Phobias," www.lynnekenney.com.
17. Paul Nussbaum, "Get to Know Your Brain." www.paulnussbaum.com.
18. Quoted in Andrew Watts, "Why Do We Develop Certain Irrational Phobias?," *Scientific American,* January 1, 2014. www.scientificamerican.com.
19. Edmund J. Bourne, *The Anxiety & Phobia Workbook*. Oakland, CA: New Harbinger, 2015.

Chapter Three: What Is It Like to Live with Phobias?

20. Emily Ford, *What You Must Think of Me: A Firsthand Account of One Teenager's Experience with Social Anxiety Disorder*. New York: Oxford, 2007.
21. Ford, *What You Must Think of Me*.
22. Ford, *What You Must Think of Me*.
23. Ford, What You Must Think of Me.
24. Quoted in Jill Martin Wrenn, "TV Stars, Travel Bloggers Not Immune to Fear of Flying," CNN, June 26, 2016. www.cnn.com.
25. Quoted in James Heflin, "Ungrounded: Beating Flying Phobia," *Valley Advocate*, May 6, 2015. http://valleyadvocate.com.

26. Quoted in Alex Preston, "Fear of Flying: The Spectre That Haunts Modern Life," *The Guardian*, December 28, 2014. www.theguardian.com.

27. Quoted in Anxiety, www.reddit.com/r/Anxiety/comments/2f9 cwz/could_someone_give_me_a_agoraphobia_success_story/.

28. Quoted in Anxiety Disorders Association of Victoria, "Ben's Story: My Recovery from Acute Anxiety and Agoraphobia," June 2004. www.adavic.org.au.

Chapter Four: Can Phobias Be Treated or Cured?

29. Quoted in Debra Smouse, "On the Subject of Fear." www.debrasmouse.com.

30. Nancy Milla, interview with the author, July 25, 2014.

31. Jeffrey Hill, interview with the author, August 16, 2016.

32. Tamar E. Chansky, *Freeing Your Child from Anxiety.* Rev. ed. New York: Random House, 2014, p. 98.

33. Christina Baker, "School-Based Mental Health Services: What Can the Partnership Look Like?," *Counseling Today*, January 1, 2013. http://ct.counseling.org.

34. Emily Hunt, interview with the author, July 18, 2016.

35. Aliana Hunt, interview with the author, July 18, 2016.

36. Aliana Hunt, interview with the author, July 18, 2016.

37. Emily Hunt, interview with the author, July 25, 2016.

38. Paul Dooley, "How to Pick the Right Anxiety Medication," Anxiety Guru. www.anxietyguru.net.

39. Richard A. Friedman, "For Fearful Fliers, a Guide to Easing the Jitters," *New York Times*, September 18, 2006. www.nytimes.com.

RECOGNIZING SIGNS OF TROUBLE

Many teens suffer in silence, too embarrassed for anyone to know about their phobia. Nearly three out of four young people fear the reactions of friends when they talk about their mental health problems. Although it may look like the teens are simply being quiet, they may be silently suffering. Help may be needed if the teen exhibits any of the following symptoms:

- Is uncomfortable talking to friends or teachers, especially ones he or she has known for a while
- Avoids eye contact, mumbles, speaks quietly or not at all when asked questions
- Blushes or trembles when in groups
- Worries excessively about doing, looking, or saying something "stupid"
- Avoids speaking up in class or during any sort of group activity
- Complains of illness and often wants to stay home from school, field trips, or parties
- Withdraws from activities, clubs, and sports and wants to spend more time at home
- Drifts away from almost all of his or her friends

If these signs are new or have increased in intensity, a close friend or family member should consider talking to the teen. Bear in mind that a person suffering from a phobia is probably not open to talking about his or her fears, so it may take some time to get him or her to open up and discuss them honestly. A doctor or health care professional will need to conduct an evaluation to see if a disorder is present.

The following organizations offer help for teens and others suffering from phobias as well as detailed information about the disorders.

Adolescent Wellness Portal

www.adolescentwellness.org

The Adolescent Wellness Portal promotes mental health and wellness in teens. Its goal is for every youth to get through adolescence without developing symptoms of anxiety or depression. It also offers resources for schools and parents regarding adolescent mental health and wellness.

American Academy of Child & Adolescent Psychiatry (AACAP)

3615 Wisconsin Ave. NW
Washington, DC 20016
www.aacap.org

Part of the mission of the AACAP is to promote the healthy development of children, adolescents, and families through advocacy, education, and research. It offers articles on mental health specifically written for teens and gives detailed, helpful ways teens can advocate for and drive their own medical health needs.

Anxiety and Depression Association of America (ADAA)

8701 Georgia Ave., Suite 412
Silver Spring, MD 20910
www.adaa.org

The ADAA promotes the prevention and cure of anxiety disorders and works to improve the lives of those affected by them. On its website, visitors can take a quiz to gauge anxiety, learn how to determine if a doctor is a good match, search for a licensed therapist, and more.

Freedom from Fear

308 Seaview Ave.
Staten Island, NY 10305
www.freedomfromfear.org

Freedom from Fear is a national not-for-profit mental health advocacy association. Its mission is to positively impact the lives of those affected by anxiety, depression, and related disorders through advocacy, education, research, and community support. It offers a treatment program designed for kids.

KidsHealth

www.kidshealth.org

The KidsHealth website has a section dedicated to teens that covers a wide variety of health and mental health issues. It is run by the nonprofit Nemours Center for Children's Health Media and provides accurate, up-to-date health information written in teen-friendly language.

National Institute of Mental Health (NIMH)

6001 Executive Blvd.
Room 6200, MSC 9663
Bethesda, MD 20892
www.nimh.nih.gov

The NIMH is the lead federal agency for research on mental disorders. Its mission is to transform the understanding and treatment of mental illnesses through basic and clinical research, paving the way for prevention, recovery, and cure.

Panic Support 4 U

www.panicsupport4u.com

Panic Support 4 U is an online support group, available 24/7, for sufferers of anxiety, panic disorders, and agoraphobia. It offers tools, coping techniques, and a community of support.

Social Anxiety Association

http://socialphobia.org

The Social Anxiety Association runs programs online and around the United States to help people overcome social anxiety. It serves as a resource and information center for matters related to social anxiety and encourages effective treatment options.

Stage of Life

www.stageoflife.com

This teen social site has a page dedicated to teens overcoming fear. Includes data and trends as well as survey results and essays submitted by teens and college students. Students from around the country share stories on how they overcame personal fears.

FOR FURTHER RESEARCH

Books

Jed Baker, *Overcoming Anxiety in Children & Teens*. Arlington, TX: New Horizons, 2015.

Edmund J. Bourne, *The Anxiety and Phobia Workbook*. Oakland, CA: New Harbinger, 2015.

Rita Carter, *The Human Brain*. New York: 2014.

Natasha Daniels, *Anxiety Sucks! A Teen Survival Guide*. Create-Space Independent Publishing Platform, 2016.

Lisa M. Schab, *The Anxiety Workbook for Teens: Activities to Help You Deal with Anxiety and Worry.* Oakland, CA: New Harbinger, 2008.

Bob Stahl and Wendy Millstine, *Calming the Rush of Panic: A Mindfulness-Based Stress Reduction Guide*. Oakland, CA: New Harbinger, 2013.

Andrea Umbach, *Conquer Your Fears and Phobias for Teens: How to Build Courage and Stop Fear from Holding You Back*. Oakland, CA: New Harbinger, 2015.

Internet Sources

KidsHealth, "Fears and Phobias." http://kidshealth.org/en/teens/phobias.html.

Massachusetts General Hospital, "Phobias."www.massgeneral.org/conditions/condition.aspx?id=370&display=about_this _condition.

Mayo Clinic, "Phobias: Definition." www.mayoclinic.org/diseases-conditions/phobias/basics/definition/con-20023478.

Lisa Miller, "Listening to Xanax," *New York Magazine,* March 2012. http://nymag.com/news/features/xanax-2012-3/index1.html.

Psychologist Anywhere Anytime, "Fears and Phobias." www.psychologistanywhereanytime.com/phobias_psychologist_and_psychologists/psychologist_fears_and_phobias.htm.

US National Library of Medicine, "Phobias," Medline Plus. https://medlineplus.gov/phobias.html.

INDEX

Note: Boldface page numbers indicate illustrations.

early intervention, 51
medication, 48, 57, 59–64
seeking sooner, 41–42
support animals, 57–58, **59**
therapy, 9–10, 48, 52–57
virtual reality, 61

Umbach, Andrea, 7
US Food and Drug
  Administration (FDA),
  59–60

Valium, 61, 63

Venustraphobia, 21
virtual reality, 61
Virtual Reality Medical Center,
  61
vomiting, fear of, 20

war, 33–34
What You Must Think of Me
  (Ford), 39–40

Xanax, 61

Yildirim, Caglar, 22

PICTURE CREDITS

Bitsy Kemper is the author of fifteen books for the very young up to young adult. She has appeared on CNN and on radio and television programs across the country. She has also been featured in hundreds of newspapers and magazines. Kemper grew up in New York, earned bachelor of art and bachelor of science degrees in North Carolina, and then earned a master's degree in California, where she and her family live happily today.